GW00499782

2023 Sweary Planner

2023
SWEARY
PLANNER

Dedicated to Dale, who ...

(1) works in Cirencester Jobcentre,
(2) I was talking to when I came up with the idea for this planner,
(3) I thought I'd dedicated the planner to LAST year but got her name completely wrong and called her "Stacey" instead, which sounds absolutely fuck all like Dale,
(4) will not be sharing in any of the profits from it because if I could afford to do that then I wouldn't need to be talking to anyone in the fucking Jobcentre for TWO YEARS, would I?

2023

January

M		2	9	16	23	30
T		3	10	17	24	31
W		4	11	18	25
T		5	12	19	26
F		6	13	20	27
S		7	14	21	28
S	1	8	15	22	29

February

M		6	13	20	27
T		7	14	21	28
W	1	8	15	22
T	2	9	16	23
F	3	10	17	24
S	4	11	18	25
S	5	12	19	26

March

M		6	13	20	27
T		7	14	21	28
W	1	8	15	22	29
T	2	9	16	23	30
F	3	10	17	24	31
S	4	11	18	25
S	5	12	19	26

April

M		3	10	17	24
T		4	11	18	25
W		5	12	19	26
T		6	13	20	27
F		7	14	21	28
S	1	8	15	22	29
S	2	9	16	23	30

May

M	1	8	15	22	29
T	2	9	16	23	30
W	3	10	17	24	31
T	4	11	18	25
F	5	12	19	26
S	6	13	20	27
S	7	14	21	28

June

M		5	12	19	26
T		6	13	20	27
W		7	14	21	28
T	1	8	15	22	29
F	2	9	16	23	30
S	3	10	17	24
S	4	11	18	25

July

M		3	10	17	24	31
T		4	11	18	25
W		5	12	19	26
T		6	13	20	27
F		7	14	21	28
S	1	8	15	22	29
S	2	9	16	23	30

August

M		7	14	21	28
T	1	8	15	22	29
W	2	9	16	23	30
T	3	10	17	24	31
F	4	11	18	25
S	5	12	19	26
S	6	13	20	27

September

M		4	11	18	25
T		5	12	19	26
W		6	13	20	27
T		7	14	21	28
F	1	8	15	22	29
S	2	9	16	23	30
S	3	10	17	24

October

M		2	9	16	23	30
T		3	10	17	24	31
W		4	11	18	25
T		5	12	19	26
F		6	13	20	27
S		7	14	21	28
S	1	8	15	22	29

November

M		6	13	20	27
T		7	14	21	28
W	1	8	15	22	29
T	2	9	16	23	30
F	3	10	17	24
S	4	11	18	25
S	5	12	19	26

December

M		4	11	18	25
T		5	12	19	26
W		6	13	20	27
T		7	14	21	28
F	1	8	15	22	29
S	2	9	16	23	30
S	3	10	17	24	31

2023, the year in which *Endgame* is set. Who was your favourite superhero? Thor? Black Panther? Scarlet Witch? Be honest, it was Thanos, wasn't it? Because we all secretly hate half the people we know and wish they'd fucking disappear, don't we?

2024

January
M	1	8	15	22	29
T	2	9	16	23	30
W	3	10	17	24	31
T	4	11	18	25	
F	5	12	19	26	
S	6	13	20	27	
S	7	14	21	28	

February
M		5	12	19	26
T		6	13	20	27
W		7	14	21	28
T	1	8	15	22	29
F	2	9	16	23	
S	3	10	17	24	
S	4	11	18	25	

March
M		4	11	18	25
T		5	12	19	26
W		6	13	20	27
T		7	14	21	28
F	1	8	15	22	29
S	2	9	16	23	30
S	3	10	17	24	31

April
M	1	8	15	22	29
T	2	9	16	23	30
W	3	10	17	24	
T	4	11	18	25	
F	5	12	19	26	
S	6	13	20	27	
S	7	14	21	28	

May
M		6	13	20	27
T		7	14	21	28
W	1	8	15	22	29
T	2	9	16	23	30
F	3	10	17	24	31
S	4	11	18	25	
S	5	12	19	26	

June
M		3	10	17	24
T		4	11	18	25
W		5	12	19	26
T		6	13	20	27
F		7	14	21	28
S	1	8	15	22	29
S	2	9	16	23	30

July
M	1	8	15	22	29
T	2	9	16	23	30
W	3	10	17	24	31
T	4	11	18	25	
F	5	12	19	26	
S	6	13	20	27	
S	7	14	21	28	

August
M		5	12	19	26
T		6	13	20	27
W		7	14	21	28
T	1	8	15	22	29
F	2	9	16	23	30
S	3	10	17	24	31
S	4	11	18	25	

September
M		2	9	16	23	30
T		3	10	17	24	
W		4	11	18	25	
T		5	12	19	26	
F		6	13	20	27	
S		7	14	21	28	
S	1	8	15	22	29	

October
M		7	14	21	28
T	1	8	15	22	29
W	2	9	16	23	30
T	3	10	17	24	31
F	4	11	18	25	
S	5	12	19	26	
S	6	13	20	27	

November
M		4	11	18	25
T		5	12	19	26
W		6	13	20	27
T		7	14	21	28
F	1	8	15	22	29
S	2	9	16	23	30
S	3	10	17	24	

December
M		2	9	16	23	30
T		3	10	17	24	31
W		4	11	18	25	
T		5	12	19	26	
F		6	13	20	27	
S		7	14	21	28	
S	1	8	15	22	29	

DECEMBER 2022

Monday
26

Tuesday
27

Wednesday
28

Thursday
29

Friday
30

Saturday
31

Sunday
1

JANUARY'S JUST A BIT SHIT REALLY

The weather is miserable, you've got no money, it's got 31 fucking days that go on forever. And your mates have turned into smug twats banging on and on about Dry January, which surely is really in reference to the fact that nobody's getting any action. BECAUSE January is the month where people are most likely to separate or file for divorce. Let's face it — after a Christmas cooped up at home with some lazy fucker who won't do their share of the food prep, cooking, or washing up, does all their bloody Christmas shopping on Christmas Eve while you're taking care of everything else, then gets totally drunk while you deal with their parents, who can blame you? Lawyers even call the first Monday back after the holidays "Divorce Day." In fact, thinking about it, January is the month when my own father walked out — he literally said he was going to the pub and never came back. So yeah. Let's see what utter bullshit this January holds.

Monday
2

Tuesday
3

Wednesday
4

Thursday
5

Friday

6

Saturday

7

Sunday

8

TAKING THE BLOODY CHRISTMAS DECS DOWN

Tradition has it that you take the decs down by January 6th. And your superstitious mother will spend every day from bloody Boxing Day harrassing you to make sure you don't forget. Remember the utterly shite year you had when you broke multiple bones, got an incurable illness, and a scammer conned you out of your savings? Oh that was definitely all due to the fact that you left your Christmas tree up ONE extra fucking day. Get the bloody thing down as soon as possible if only to stop the harrassment. Somehow this pain-in-the-ass task gets allocated to the most useless member of any household, because the general consensus is that they have to do SOMETHING to make up for being a lazy fucker all through Christmas. But if you leave them unsupervised then they'll break half the baubles, stab themselves with multiple pine needles, and strangle the cat with the fairy lights. Although that WOULD save on extortionate vet bills. Which nobody needs after Christmas, let's face it.

JANUARY 2023

Monday

9

Tuesday

10

Wednesday

11

Thursday

12

Friday
13

Saturday
14

Sunday
15

HOW FUCKING AWFUL HAS YOUR WEEK BEEN?
Write up your Fucking Awful week, then post it on the Sweary Planner's Facebook page.

JANUARY 2023

Monday

16

Tuesday

17

Wednesday

18

Thursday

19

Friday
20

Saturday
21

Sunday
22

HOW FUCKING AWFUL HAS YOUR WEEK BEEN?
Write up your Fucking Awful week, then post it on the Sweary Planner's Facebook page.

JANUARY 2023

Monday
23

Tuesday
24

Wednesday
25

Thursday
26

Friday
27

Saturday
28

Sunday
29

HOW FUCKING AWFUL HAS YOUR WEEK BEEN?

Write up your Fucking Awful week, then post it on the Sweary Planner's Facebook page.

Monday
30

Tuesday
31

Don't forget to go to the game at the back of this planner to check your score — see how much of a Fucking Awful Year you're having already!

Wednesday
1

Thursday
2

Friday

3

Saturday

4

Sunday

5

FAILURE FEBRUARY

February is the month of FAILURE. Whatever you've tried to do so far this year to improve your ability to do life like a NORMAL fucking adult just hasn't worked, has it? You're even fucking up the basics. Tried to stop drinking only to get in the habit of singlehandedly consuming a bottle of bubbly when the kids head off to school. Or tried to stop smoking only to get through half a pack because you know the little fuckers COME BACK HOME. Tried healthier eating only to spend every night eating the leftover Christmas pudding because, you know, you hate wasting food. Tried to get fit but it's too bloody cold out there, and icy, and dark, and full of smug twats running around in their neon tops with tits that DON'T hit them in the face. You didn't keep any of your New Year's Resolutions whatsoever and you blocked that friend who very publicly did because you couldn't trust yourself not to comment by telling them to take their homemade vegan gluten-free dairy-free sugar-free fucking taste-free SHIT pie and stick it up their arse!

FEBRUARY 2023

Monday

6

Tuesday

7

Wednesday

8

Thursday

9

Friday
10

Saturday
11

Sunday
12

HOW FUCKING AWFUL HAS YOUR WEEK BEEN?

Write up your Fucking Awful week, then post it on the Sweary Planner's Facebook page.

FEBRUARY 2023

Monday
13

Tuesday
14

Wednesday
15

Thursday
16

Friday
17

Saturday
18

Sunday
19

VALENTINE'S DAY

What a load of shit. Shops full of red crap, chocolates are twice the price just because the packaging is pink, and whole supermarket aisles are dedicated to tacky cards that don't reflect the reality of wasting years of your life with an arsehole who was likely shagging your ex-best friend the whole time. Thank fuck you're single and never putting up with that shit again. If only you could ignore the constant BOMBARDMENT of Valentine's junk from fucking Amazon or your personal stalker, aka Facebook, you could quite happily ignore the whole thing. Except your well-meaning aunt sends you flowers because she doesn't want you to end up as lonely as she is, but that only makes you wonder if that might be your destiny. And if you're in a relationship, well, you FUCKED IT UP on the very first Valentine's Day when you wore expensive lingerie and cooked them their favourite meal. With SEVEN courses. Followed by a bit of bum fun. NOTHING will beat that. Now you mark Valentine's Day by purchasing some leg-wax strips from Poundland.

FEBRUARY 2023

Monday
20

Tuesday
21

Wednesday
22

Thursday
23

Friday
24

Saturday
25

Sunday
26

HOW FUCKING AWFUL HAS YOUR WEEK BEEN?

Write up your Fucking Awful week, then post it on the Sweary Planner's Facebook page.

Monday
27

Tuesday
28

Don't forget to go to the game at the back of this planner to check your score — see how much of a Fucking Awful Year you're having already!

Wednesday
1

Thursday
2

Friday
3

Saturday
4

Sunday
5

MISLEADING MARCH

March is supposedly "Optimism Month," where you focus on being positive, thankful, and appreciative of everything the world has to offer. Where you convince yourself that a brighter, happier future is REALLY possible, and maybe only a matter of days away. March is the month where spring is in the air, flowers start to bloom, and animals are coming out of hibernation. It promises that hope and love and joy are just waiting for you. It brings you a few days of a speck of blue sky so you dare to believe that all this optimism is oh so POWERFUL and you are AT ONE with the world at last! You are filled with the hope that the winter has finally gone and with enough daylight and sunlight you CAN BE ALL YOU DREAM OF. But then it absolutely pisses down with rain for the entire month, and the only animals you see are the fucking slugs fighting their way to destroy the few plants that are actually making the effort to blossom in the remaining bits of your garden you didn't pave over because you couldn't be arsed with it anymore.

Monday
6

Tuesday
7

Wednesday
8

Thursday
9

Friday
10

Saturday
11

Sunday
12

HOW FUCKING AWFUL HAS YOUR WEEK BEEN?
Write up your Fucking Awful week, then post it on the Sweary Planner's Facebook page.

MARCH 2023

Monday
13

Tuesday
14

Wednesday
15

Thursday
16

Friday
17

Saturday
18

Sunday
19

WORLD SLEEP DAY — MARCH 17th

A celebration of sleep, a call to action around sleep issues and research, and an awareness of sleep conditions. That's what World Sleep Day is all about. How about we make it a day where inconsiderate twats keep their stupid little arguments INdoors during the day and not right outside your bedroom window at 3 in the morning. Or one where the 4am bin collectors don't upturn the glass recycling at a massive height to make the entire contents smash into the truck. Or maybe your dog doesn't wake you by vomiting all over your fucking pillow right next to your head. And why is it that you feel so utterly SHIT if you don't have a decent night's sleep? It's like having a hangover, a lobotomy, and jetlag all at the same time, making you completely unable to navigate life and increasing the likelihood of you being violent, especially with those noisy fucking neighbours. Now that would be an interesting sleep study ... how many crimes have been committed just because someone didn't have a decent fucking night's sleep?

Monday
20

Tuesday
21

Wednesday
22

Thursday
23

Friday
24

Saturday
25

Sunday
26

HOW FUCKING AWFUL HAS YOUR WEEK BEEN?
Write up your Fucking Awful week, then post it on the Sweary Planner's Facebook page.

Monday
27

Tuesday
28

Wednesday
29

Thursday
30

Friday
31

You're a quarter of the way through 2023! Don't forget to go to the game at the back of this planner to check your score — see how much of a Fucking Awful Year you're having already!

Saturday
1

Sunday
2

APRIL'S ASSHOLES

The fiscal year ends. And April is the month where anyone that is an asshole about money is going to take their assholery to an entirely new level. Your self-employed ex against whom you have a restraining order will be lying through their back teeth about how much money they earn purely so they can pay as little as legally possible to feed and clothe their own kids, yet simultaneously be booking a luxury holiday and banging on about their amazing parenting skills. School administrators will be working out just how far they can cut the arts department's budget, and wondering how much more money they can coerce the previously enthusiastic now resentful head of the PTA into raising (she used to be really senior in a major corporation until she gave it up to bake fucking brownies to make money for educational necessities). And governments all over the world will start their sneaky little plans to see just how much further they can fuck up their respective country's educational, health, and social care services. Ass. Holes.

APRIL 2023

Monday
3

Tuesday
4

Wednesday
5

Thursday
6

Friday
7

Saturday
8

Sunday
9

HOW FUCKING AWFUL HAS YOUR WEEK BEEN?
Write up your Fucking Awful week, then post it on the Sweary Planner's Facebook page.

APRIL 2023

Monday
10

Tuesday
11

Wednesday
12

Thursday
13

Friday
14

Saturday
15

Sunday
16

INTERNATIONAL BE KIND TO LAWYERS DAY

They're absolute fuckers. Such fuckers, they even need a day where every single person, in every single country, needs to be told to be fucking kind to them. On April 12th, spare a thought for that money-grabbing prick who made a fucking fortune out of your divorce. Or that asshole who defends the perpetrators of heinous crimes and convinces themselves that even the biggest fuckers deserve someone to defend them. Do they even give a shit about whether their client is telling the truth or lying through their back teeth? Fuck no. Do they remotely care about being right or wrong? Fair and just? Again, fuck no. Their entire existence is dependent on winning, at whatever cost, usually yours, except they won't even take you on unless you've got a shitload of money lying around anyway. What other professions will happily charge you per fucking minute of their time? Let's get rid of this corrupt 12th-century system and allow the public to decide who to let off from being an absolute fucker — oh we already do. It's called reality TV.

Monday

17

Tuesday

18

Wednesday

19

Thursday

20

Friday
21

Saturday
22

Sunday
23

HOW FUCKING AWFUL HAS YOUR WEEK BEEN?
Write up your Fucking Awful week, then post it on the Sweary Planner's Facebook page.

APRIL 2023

Monday
24

Tuesday
25

Wednesday
26

Thursday
27

Friday
28

Saturday
29

Sunday
30

Was April totally shit? Don't forget to go to the game at the back of this planner to check your score —
see how much of a Fucking Awful Year you're having already!

HOW FUCKING AWFUL HAS YOUR WEEK BEEN?

Write up your Fucking Awful week, then post it on the Sweary Planner's Facebook page.

MAY 2023

Monday

1

Tuesday

2

Wednesday

3

Thursday

4

Friday
5

Saturday
6

Sunday
7

MAY AWARENESS OVERLOAD MONTH

May has apparently got the most number of "awareness" themes. What is it with that? In the UK alone there are events planned this May to create awareness of strokes, walking, storytelling, local history (with a specific day dedicated to mills, would you believe), deafness, donkeys, dying, mental health, foster care, allergies, vegetarians, weaning, numbers(?), firefighters, sunbathing (from a dermatology perspective because you can't rely on there being any actual sun in England this time of year), and baking for asthma. Just baking isn't good enough, it seems ... but baking for ASTHMA is entirely acceptable. There's a day, week, or month dedicated to all sorts of things that are supposed to increase our empathy and understanding of a previously unheard of cause, but that just end up annoying the shit out of us. Every time someone changes their social media frame to include one ribbon or another, the only thing it increases is the urge to strangle the social media friend with that ribbon.

MAY 2023

Monday
8

Tuesday
9

Wednesday
10

Thursday
11

Friday
12

Saturday
13

Sunday
14

HOW FUCKING AWFUL HAS YOUR WEEK BEEN?
Write up your Fucking Awful week, then post it on the Sweary Planner's Facebook page.

MAY 2023

Monday
15

Tuesday
16

Wednesday
17

Thursday
18

Friday
19

Saturday
20

Sunday
21

INTERNATIONAL DAY OF FAMILIES

In the '90s, May 15th was decreed by the United Nations as a day to recognise all things relating to families. Obviously someone was completely oblivious to the fact that, by then, everyone was living in such dysfunction that "family" was becoming just another f-word. How would most people spend International Day of Families? Ignore the racist, inappropriate grandfather? Stay well away from the pervy old uncle and his enabling mother? Maybe that's how the House of Windsor might navigate it. If they're not spewing their guts on global television. Not unlike the rest of us really, whose fucked up family members appear on Jerry Springer. Oh, and look what special occasion appears just two days later ... World Telecommunication and Information Society Day. Because if your family isn't fully fucked up yet, it sure as shit will be once every member has a digital device they can sit staring at during every social gathering.

MAY 2023

Monday
22

Tuesday
23

Wednesday
24

Thursday
25

Friday
26

Saturday
27

Sunday
28

HOW FUCKING AWFUL HAS YOUR WEEK BEEN?
Write up your Fucking Awful week, then post it on the Sweary Planner's Facebook page.

Monday
29

Tuesday
30

Wednesday
31

Don't forget to go to the game at the back of this planner to check your score — see how much of a Fucking Awful Year you're having already!

Thursday
1

Friday
2

Saturday
3

Sunday
4

BRIDAL BULLSHIT SEASON COMMENCES

You know it's coming. All the bridal bullshit. The wedding invitation has been oozing smugness since the moment it landed with a thud through your letterbox, heavy with precise instructions regarding who, when, what, why, and how. Probably ending up costing you more than the engagement ring did. It starts with the overly elaborate oh soooo looooong bachelorette weekend away in some picturesque European spa resort that you pay a bloody fortune to go on in honour of an old friend, only to discover that you have absolutely nothing whatsoever in common with any of her new friends but you have to grin and bear it, much like you're having to do with the plastic tube that's been shoved up your rectum in order to pump mycotoxin-free coffee through your bowels. Whatever happened to a good old-fashioned hen night where you're kicked out of a bar, and end up in a club at the dodgy end of town where you get off with a bouncer followed by a fellow bridesmaid, then stagger home at 11am minus a shoe?

JUNE 2023

Monday
5

Tuesday
6

Wednesday
7

Thursday
8

Friday
9

Saturday
10

Sunday
11

HOW FUCKING AWFUL HAS YOUR WEEK BEEN?
Write up your Fucking Awful week, then post it on the Sweary Planner's Facebook page.

JUNE 2023

Monday
12

Tuesday
13

Wednesday
14

Thursday
15

Friday
16

Saturday
17

Sunday
18

INTERNATIONAL PICNIC DAY — 18th JUNE

One of the most overrated activities in the world. You grab a mouldy blanket from the boot of your car, lay it on top of some dried up animal faeces, and attempt to spread out what was a delicious meal that has since got totally soaked with the flask of coffee that's leaked all over everything. You drop your phone in a stream while trying to take a photo in order to pretend to your Fakebook friends that you're actually having a wonderfully romantic time, get attacked by a swan that you can't fight back because the locals will call the police while filming you beating up a protected creature, and in desperation, pee behind a tree without realising until it's too late that you're hovering in the middle of a shitload of stinging nettles. The only actual joy you have is when you catch sight of the bastard dog who stole your entire fucking pack of gourmet prosciutto, shitting it out a couple of hours later while its asshole owners — who did fuck all to stop the little thief — try to clean treacle-turd off their brand new picnic blanket.

JUNE 2023

Monday
19

Tuesday
20

Wednesday
21

Thursday
22

Friday
23

Saturday
24

Sunday
25

HOW FUCKING AWFUL HAS YOUR WEEK BEEN?
Write up your Fucking Awful week, then post it on the Sweary Planner's Facebook page.

JUNE 2023

Monday
26

Tuesday
27

Wednesday
28

Thursday
29

Friday
30

You're halfway through 2023! Well done for hanging in. Don't forget to go to the game at the back of this planner to check your score — see how much of a Fucking Awful Year you're having already!

Saturday
1

Sunday
2

SUMMER HOLIDAY HELL

In just a few weeks the kids will be off school — a time eagerly anticipated by parents and offspring alike, and absolutely fucking dreaded by everyone else. Grandparents are tempted to book a long ... very long ... holiday, in a place that's really, really far away, that no, darling, you can't come and visit, but who wants to take the risk of spending all that money on a holiday only to find the resort is packed full of other people's grandchildren? Instead they contemplate faking their own deaths. And the blissfully childfree start collecting egg cartons to stick all over the walls in a vain attempt to muffle the noise of the neighbourhood kids setting up multiple paddling pools in the communal garden and screaming every fucking day for six weeks. Within 24 hours of the school gates closing for the summer, even the parents themselves are wondering why the hell they didn't book their little darlings into an army cadet camp and invite that really hot science teacher around for a threesome instead.

JULY 2023

Monday
3

Tuesday
4

Wednesday
5

Thursday
6

Friday
7

Saturday
8

Sunday
9

HOW FUCKING AWFUL HAS YOUR WEEK BEEN?
Write up your Fucking Awful week, then post it on the Sweary Planner's Facebook page.

JULY 2023

Monday
10

Tuesday
11

Wednesday
12

Thursday
13

Friday
14

Saturday
15

Sunday
16

CHEER UP THE LONELY DAY (USA) — July 11th

Some do-gooder came up with this day to encourage people to spend time with old gits stuck on their own in homes without anyone visiting them. Ever wondered why nobody wants to visit them? Because they probably spent their entire lives being such fuckers to their in-laws, their kids, and their grandkids that everyone would much rather prefer to pretend they'd corked it. Sure, there might be a random neighbour from somewhere who pops in all smiley but that's only because they're sniffing around to see if there's a chance of inheriting something. And the old git knows it. These old people don't need to be cheered up. They need to have not been such selfish assholes during their lifetime. Or have a decent enough will so that their spawn might want to spend some time with them. Or maybe they've had it sussed all along and are actually quite happy that nobody comes to visit them so they can live out their later years in peace and fucking quiet, wanking away under the pretext of having dementia.

JULY 2023

Monday
17

Tuesday
18

Wednesday
19

Thursday
20

Friday
21

Saturday
22

Sunday
23

HOW FUCKING AWFUL HAS YOUR WEEK BEEN?
Write up your Fucking Awful week, then post it on the Sweary Planner's Facebook page.

JULY 2023

Monday
24

Tuesday
25

Wednesday
26

Thursday
27

Friday
28

Saturday
29

Sunday
30

HOW FUCKING AWFUL HAS YOUR WEEK BEEN?

Write up your Fucking Awful week, then post it on the Sweary Planner's Facebook page.

Monday
31

Don't forget to go to the game at the back of this planner to check your score — see how much of a Fucking Awful Year you're having already!

Tuesday
1

Wednesday
2

Thursday
3

Friday

4

Saturday

5

Sunday

6

ALL THOSE FUCKING FESTIVALS

August is the month of one bloody festival after another. And against your better judgement, one of your "fun-loving" mates persuaded you to go with them. You've inexplicably loaded up your car with more stuff for a weekend in a muddy field than you knew you had. You've moved HOUSE with less shit before. You queue for hours to get into the bloody thing, then walk back and forth at least six times lugging crap, by which time you're definitely less inclined to put up a tent but instead more inclined to whack your annoyingly enthusiastic friend over the head with a tent pole and stick a tent peg in their eye. IF you do manage to get the tent up, it's bound to have pissed down the whole time so you and all your belongings, including your mobile phone, are soaked through. Although the phone doesn't really matter because at some point you'll forget it's in your pocket and it will end up at the bottom of a portaloo covered in other people's shit. This entire weekend will cost you the equaivalent of a month's mortgage.

AUGUST 2023

Monday

7

Tuesday

8

Wednesday

9

Thursday

10

Friday
11

Saturday
12

Sunday
13

HAPPINESS HAPPENS DAY (USA) — AUGUST 8th

What's more irritating that a ridiculously happy person? A fucking group of them. Dedicated to smiling their simple fucking smiles and spreading their poxy fucking positivity, as if that's going to make any fucking difference to the rest of us, who wake up knowing full well that it's all downhill from here on. Even if you do wake up feeling remotely optimistic, it's only a matter of time before some twat pisses you off, usually by posting about their perfect fucking life on social media, which you know for a fact is total bollocks because just the night before you listened to them bawl their eyes out about how their job is shit, they've got fuck-all money, and they haven't had sex in months. But today they're out spreading fucking joy and making "happiness happen." The only thing that makes happy people more annoying is if they've got fucking spaniels with them, wagging their stupid bloody tails because they're so excited about a ball, a stick, a leaf, some piss up a wall, or another dog's asshole.

AUGUST 2023

Monday
14

Tuesday
15

Wednesday
16

Thursday
17

Friday
18

Saturday
19

Sunday
20

HOW FUCKING AWFUL HAS YOUR WEEK BEEN?
Write up your Fucking Awful week, then post it on the Sweary Planner's Facebook page.

Monday
21

Tuesday
22

Wednesday
23

Thursday
24

Friday
25

Saturday
26

Sunday
27

HOW FUCKING AWFUL HAS YOUR WEEK BEEN?
Write up your Fucking Awful week, then post it on the Sweary Planner's Facebook page.

AUGUST 2023

Monday
28

Tuesday
29

Wednesday
30

Thursday
31

You're heading into the year's final third. Keep going. Don't forget to go to the game at the back of this planner to check your score — see how much of a Fucking Awful Year you're having already!

Friday

1

Saturday

2

Sunday

3

SEPTEMBER SUCKS

The evenings are drawing in, the kids go back to school, and you can settle into that lovely quiet, calm space after the summer but before the winter until you spot THAT shelf in your local supermarket. The fucking Christmas shelf. WHAAAAAT?!!!!!! You're still wearing shorts. And eating salads. And topping up your tan because there's an occasional sunny day. The heating's not on yet. You haven't got your Halloween costume sorted. Who the bloody hell is thinking about Christmas in September? Yes, such psychopaths exist, and as soon as you spot that first Christmas shelf, suddenly you see the C-word pop up everywhere: a selection of seasonal greetings cards next to the birthday cards, parents and in-laws start their annual passive-aggressive attack over who's hosting who, there's a weird TV commercial with a smug-faced, chiffon-clad celebrity that MIGHT be advertising perfume but it's anyone's guess really, and some fucking lunatic in The Cotswolds starts pickling Brussels sprouts.

SEPTEMBER 2023

Monday
4

Tuesday
5

Wednesday
6

Thursday
7

Friday
8

Saturday
9

Sunday
10

HOW FUCKING AWFUL HAS YOUR WEEK BEEN?
Write up your Fucking Awful week, then post it on the Sweary Planner's Facebook page.

SEPTEMBER 2023

Monday
11

Tuesday
12

Wednesday
13

Thursday
14

Friday
15

Saturday
16

Sunday
17

HOW FUCKING AWFUL HAS YOUR WEEK BEEN?

Write up your Fucking Awful week, then post it on the Sweary Planner's Facebook page.

SEPTEMBER 2023

Monday
18

Tuesday
19

Wednesday
20

Thursday
21

Friday
22

Saturday
23

Sunday
24

INTERNATIONAL DAY OF PEACE — SEPTEMBER 21st

A day when global leaders are supposed to promote peaceful acts, encourage kind and caring behaviour, and not fire any weapons at each other. Narcissistic, manipulative, controlling assholes actually need a day in the calendar to get them to behave like decent human beings. The rest of the time it's apparently totally acceptable for them to do the exact opposite and, in fact, it's probably in the job description. Peace Day events include a minute's silence, during which you can guarantee that you'll give yourself stomach ache by holding in a massive random fart and/or try your best not to piss yourself laughing for absolutely no reason whatsoever. Football matches in the spirit of peace are also held, except nobody in their right mind would invite the English to watch one of them unless they wanted to transform it from a day honouring peace into one honouring piss: getting pissed, pissing everyone off, and taking a piss wherever you like. Not that dissimilar to some global leaders, actually.

SEPTEMBER 2023

Monday
25

Tuesday
26

Wednesday
27

Thursday
28

Friday
29

Saturday
30

Don't forget to go to the game at the back of this planner to check your score — see how much of a Fucking Awful Year you're having!

Sunday
1

OCTOBER'S WINTER FILTH

The Anglo-Saxons called October "Winterfylleth," which when you say it out loud, just about sums up the whole month. You know why? Because of all the falling leaves hiding all the dog shit that lazy fucking owners can't be arsed to pick up. Seriously, how hard is it? Not the dog shit, which won't be hard at all because all the bloody rain will have turned it into wet mush, the likes of which you'll NEVER get out of the sixty quid Merino wool gloves you've literally JUST treated yourself to, which of course you had to be wearing when you slipped on the sopping wet leaves because you're so fucking clumsy. And as for the dog poo that does actually get picked up ... how much of it actually makes it into a dog poo bin as opposed to getting casually dropped somewhere near one? Or around one. Or rested on top of one. Or perfectly balanced where it is JUST hanging out. Fucking put it INSIDE! And don't hurl it in the air to get caught on a bare branch and just hang there for weeks, like a sad saggy testicle. Put it in the fucking bin.

OCTOBER 2023

Monday
2

Tuesday
3

Wednesday
4

Thursday
5

Friday

6

Saturday

7

Sunday

8

HOW FUCKING AWFUL HAS YOUR WEEK BEEN?

Write up your Fucking Awful week, then post it on the Sweary Planner's Facebook page.

OCTOBER 2023

Monday
9

Tuesday
10

Wednesday
11

Thursday
12

Friday
13

Saturday
14

Sunday
15

HALLOWEEN'S COMING UP

What the actual fuck has happened to Halloween? Back in the day, you and your sibling would throw on some costumes from a dusty old dressing-up box, knock on a few neighbours' doors, smile sweetly, and politely accept whatever treat they'd offer you. Now there's weird orange shit everywhere, hordes of fucking kids roaming entire towns, and parents reluctantly trudging along to steer them away from (or toward) the local psychopaths. You try to get into the spirit of it by stocking up on sweets, only to have a kid visit who is allergic to fucking everything, so you spend half the night going through all the ingredients with the front door wide open, providing heating for the whole fucking neighbourhood. The little shits are all wearing the same polyester costumes, so you spend the other half wondering whether you'll get sued if one of them goes up in flames when standing too close to your candlelit pumpkin. Better off not having one, turning off all the lights, and sitting in the dark eating a shitload of Haribo in fucking peace and quiet.

OCTOBER 2023

Monday
16

Tuesday
17

Wednesday
18

Thursday
19

Friday
20

Saturday
21

Sunday
22

HOW FUCKING AWFUL HAS YOUR WEEK BEEN?
Write up your Fucking Awful week, then post it on the Sweary Planner's Facebook page.

OCTOBER 2023

Monday
23

Tuesday
24

Wednesday
25

Thursday
26

Friday
27

Saturday
28

Sunday
29

HOW FUCKING AWFUL HAS YOUR WEEK BEEN?
Write up your Fucking Awful week, then post it on the Sweary Planner's Facebook page.

OCT/NOV 2023

Monday
30

Tuesday
31

Don't forget to go to the game at the back of this planner to check your score — see how much of a Fucking Awful Year you're having!

Wednesday
1

Email caroline@carolinepover.com to see if she's bothered to make a Fucking Awful Planner for 2024.

Thursday
2

NOVEMBER 2023

Friday

3

Saturday

4

Sunday

5

NO NO NO NOVEMBER

Just no. November is such a waste of a month. You can't ACTUALLY get anything done because everyone is using Christmas as an excuse to avoid doing anything NORMAL. Try to get anyone in to do some electrical/construction/maintenance work and it's all, "Oooooh too busy now ... maybe after Christmas." Ordering a thoughtful, artisan-made treat for yourself results in "Oooooh, not until after Christmas now." Trying to get a shag in with your Christmas-obsessed other half also evokes one of the above responses. November generally sucks. And there's only about three hours of daylight. Although, the one good thing about November is Guy Fawkes Night, where British people commemorate a plot from over four hundred years ago, when an activist was caught with explosives intended to blow up the House of Lords. Let's face it, these days most of us are secretly hoping someone will do the same for certain turds in the House of Commons.

NOVEMBER 2023

Monday
6

Tuesday
7

Wednesday
8

Thursday
9

Friday
10

Saturday
11

Sunday
12

HOW FUCKING AWFUL HAS YOUR WEEK BEEN?
Write up your Fucking Awful week, then post it on the Sweary Planner's Facebook page.

NOVEMBER 2023

Monday
13

Tuesday
14

Wednesday
15

Thursday
16

Friday
17

Saturday
18

Sunday
19

FULL BEAVER MOON (USA) — NOVEMBER 27th

The November full moon is known as a Full Beaver Moon because it was traditionally the day to set beaver traps. What absolute bollocks. Everyone knows it's the time of year when you stop shaving or waxing or whatever the fuck you feel pressured to do with your bush because it's too fucking cold to keep your knickers off for any length of time and you could do with the extra insulation. Besides which, you're unlikely to get any action until New Year's Eve, and then it will be from someone who'll be too pissed to even notice let alone appreciate whether or not you spent half an hour of your time and three hours of your wages having molten hot liquid spread onto, then yanked off your asshole. So you let it all hang out, and delight in the sight of it all confidently taking over your lower region. It's developing a personality of its own. You feel it dismissing everything in its path, confidently pushing past even the strongest of underwear elastic, and in celebration of your first grey one, you name it Harriet.

NOVEMBER 2023

Monday
20

Tuesday
21

Wednesday
22

Thursday
23

Friday
24

Saturday
25

Sunday
26

HOW FUCKING AWFUL HAS YOUR WEEK BEEN?
Write up your Fucking Awful week, then post it on the Sweary Planner's Facebook page.

NOVEMBER 2023

Monday
27

Tuesday
28

Wednesday
29

Thursday
30

Nearly there! One more month to go! Don't forget to go to the game at the back of this planner, and update your score to see how much of a Fucking Awful Year you're having in 2023.

Friday

1

Saturday

2

Sunday

3

THE C-WORD

It's here. No avoiding it anymore. An entire month when the volume of Christmas music in shops will give you a severe case of tinnitus; dogs get humiliatingly walked while wearing fucking mince pie costumes; grannies arm themselves with their Zimmer frames in order to beat the shit out of anyone going near their sherry; and you stock up on Diazepam in order to survive the actual day itself. Men throughout the world spend Christmas Eve in gift shops, with a glazed look on their faces, not because they're pissed on mulled wine but because they have absolutely no idea where they are or what they're doing, until 2pm when the glazed look turns to sheer panic, and they'll buy fucking anything. Which is why your brother always gets you such utterly shite presents. Every single TV channel is showing a Christmas documentary, a Christmas cooking show, or Christmas movies about brats not getting their own way. Seriously, if I had a kid like that, I'd have left the little shit home alone too.

DECEMBER 2023

Monday
4

Tuesday
5

Wednesday
6

Thursday
7

Friday
8

Saturday
9

Sunday
10

HOW FUCKING AWFUL HAS YOUR WEEK BEEN?
Write up your Fucking Awful week, then post it on the Sweary Planner's Facebook page.

DECEMBER 2023

Monday
11

Tuesday
12

Wednesday
13

Thursday
14

Friday
15

Saturday
16

Sunday
17

HOW FUCKING AWFUL HAS YOUR WEEK BEEN?
Write up your Fucking Awful week, then post it on the Sweary Planner's Facebook page.

DECEMBER 2023

Monday
18

Tuesday
19

Wednesday
20

Thursday
21

Friday

22

Saturday

23

Sunday

24

FESTIVE FUCK-UPS

This is the week where you regret whatever the fuck you stupidly decided to do for Christmas. Whatever you chose, it will be a fucking nightmare. If you're hosting, then within minutes you're hating your fucking guests who've ensconced themselves on your favourite sofa and made it clear they're not lifting a fucking finger for the entire holidays until moments before they leave when they grab all the leftover booze to stuff into their bags. If you're a guest, then you'll end up sleeping in a teenage boy's bedroom, trying not to throw up at the stench or the spunk that the mother's tried and failed miserably to remove from the room and just pretends isn't there. If you sensibly refused to go to your fucked up family and instead decided to have a quiet one at home but offered to take care of your friend's dog while she fucked off abroad, then you can bet it pisses all over the Christmas tree, then swallows multiple decorations so that you spend your quiet one waiting for a dog to shit out a Santa.

DECEMBER 2023

Monday
25

Tuesday
26

Wednesday
27

Thursday
28

Friday
29

Saturday
30

Sunday
31

THANK FUCK THAT'S OVER

NOTES

NOTES

NOTES

NOTES

NOTES

NOTES

NOTES

HOW FUCKING AWFUL WAS YOUR 2023?

POLICE CAME TO YOUR HOUSE 2 points (triple score if they took you away with them)	PARENT DIED 8 points (minus 5 if you didn't like them anyway)	HOUSE GOT BROKEN INTO 6 points	WENT TO A&E IN AN AMBULANCE 7 points
HAD AN OPERATION 6 points (double points if against your will)	DROPPED PHONE IN TOILET 2 points (8 points if brand new)	PASSED OUT DURING AN ORGASM 1 point (triple score if it was while masturbating)	NEAR-DEATH EXPERIENCE 8 points
UNWANTED PREGNANCY 8 points (triple points if it was from the only sex you had all year)	BROKE A BONE 4 points	PET DIED 9 points	GOT CAUGHT UP IN FREAK WEATHER 2 points
GOT SOMETHING STUCK IN AN ORIFICE 4 points	DEVELOPED AN ONGOING ILLNESS 7 points	DOCTOR SAID ONGOING ILLNESS IS ALL IN MY HEAD 8 points	IN COURT WITH PSYCHOPATH 6 points (double points if they represent the government)
TARGETTED BY KNOWN FRAUDSTER 5 points (double points if you gave them money)	CAUGHT AN STD 6 points (extra 2 points if it was on your birthday)	VOMITED AND/OR HAD DIARRHOEA 2 points (double points if simultaneously)	INTERACTED WITH A LAWYER 4 points (extra point if they're your own)
ATTENDED A FUNERAL 3 points (minus 3 points if you're secretly celebrating)	MADE REDUNDANT 7 points	BECAME MATT HANCOCK'S GIRLFRIEND 10 points	SPRAINED ANKLE ON WALK 3 points (extra point per mile you had to walk home)
GOT BANNED ON SOCIAL MEDIA 1 point	BECAME ESTRANGED FROM FAMILY MEMBER 5 points	ESTRANGED FAMILY MEMBER WANTED TO RECONNECT 8 points	YOUR SCORE Score per incident, e.g., give yourself 7 points every time you were in an ambulance in 2023.

RESULTS

0–50   Your year wasn't Fucking Awful. A few shit things happened, but that's life. Stop bloody whinging.

51–99   Oooooh ... you had a bit of a rough time in 2023. But it could have been worse. Much worse.

Over 100 Fuck me! How are you still managing to function with that level of shit going on during the past twelve months?! Congratulations — your year was, without a doubt, FUCKING AWFUL.

THE SWEARY PLANNER ©Caroline Pover

To order copies of next year's planner ...
... email caroline@carolinepover.com, or
go to www.carolinepover.com, or Amazon
(that's assuming she can be arsed to do this again).

Comments and feedback ...
... are absolutely not welcome whatsoever.

Printed in Great Britain
by Amazon

13493555R00071